SAPPHO DOES HAY(NA)KU

ALSO BY SCOTT KEENEY

Above the Surface (with Rachel Archelaus)

Early Returns

Pickpocket Poetica

Walloping Shrug

SAPPHO DOES HAY(NA)KU

SCOTT KEENEY

Sephyrus Press
UNBOUNDED

Sappho Does Hay(na)ku
Copyright © 2006, 2008, 2018 by Scott Keeney

Illustrations by Jennifer Pesavento
Book design by Scott Keeney
Typeset in Brioso Pro

978-1-948728-02-7 Paperback
978-1-948728-03-4 Ebook

PUBLICATION HISTORY
First Ebook Edition, June 2006
Hand-bound Limited Edition, September 2008
Revised and Expanded Edition, 2018

Some of the poems in this book originally appeared in *Melancholia's Tremulous Dreadlocks*, *Secrets*, and *Joe Brainard's Pyjamas*.

CONTENTS

Sappho Does Hay(na)ku	1
Dear Hera	3
Aphrodite of the Flowers at Knossos	4
Philosophy	5
Beautiful Women ...	6
Arrows of Eros	7
What To Do?	8
No Harbor	9
Promise	10
Invitation	11
Lament	12
Mighty Aphrodite	13
Eros, Come On,	14
Rash	15
Chaste Artemis	16
Hesperos	17
Theme	18
Miss Scarlet	19
Nightingale	20
Enough	21
Two Doves	22
Dawn	23
Advice for a Girl	24
To a Young Love	26
Vista	27
Chamber Peeking	28
Virgin I	29
Virgin II	30
Moon Honey Drift	32
End of the Night	33
By Myself	35
Emptiness	36
Morning Wood	37

Love Gusts	38
To Eros	39
Late	40
Love	41
Oh	42
On Earth	43
In Truth	44
To a Charmer	45
Choosing	46
Handsome Guy	47
Flirting	48
Peek-a-Boo	49
Reunion	50
Fury	51
The Ring	52
Head's Up	53
Andromeda	54
Poor Girl	56
Graces, Muses	57
Parting Gift	58
Strangers in the Night	59
Lyric for Lesbos	60
Hurt	61
The Swallow	62
A Column of Good Things	63
Some Gift	64
Sandal	65
Garment	66
Vision	67
Entering the Black of Sleep	68
Dialogue	69
Good Morning	71
Sleep	72
Tainted Love	73
Old Pro	74

Grief Counselor	75
Old Age	76
The World Does Not End	77
The World Does Not End	78
Hermes and the River	81
Sweet Girl	82
Re: the Gods	83
On Beauty and Age	84
On Beauty and Age	85
On Beauty and Age	86
On Beauty and Age	87
On Beauty and Age	88
Youth of Today	89
Appreciation	90
Desire and Sun	91
Sappho Does	**93**
Sappho Writes Again	**103**
Sing/Sung	105
Implication	106
Aphrodite, My Lady	107
Girlfriend	108
Epithalamium	109
My Word	110
Beautiful	111
Remember	112
A Gift for Aphrodite	113
A Gift for Aphrodite II	114
Mirror Effect	115
Leda's Egg	116
Long Time	117
Wrapped	118
A Wandering	119
Close	120

SAPPHO DOES HAY(NA)KU

DEAR HERA

Sailed
to your island.
Nice shrine.

APHRODITE OF THE FLOWERS AT KNOSSOS

Shadows
branches weave
across the brook—

enter
my temple
of apple trees.

Windblown
white blossoms,
grazing brown mare—

honey
gold wine,
overfill my cup.

PHILOSOPHY

    Three
    naked girls
    shave their legs

    around
    a wellspring
    in the moonlight.

BEAUTIFUL WOMEN...

dancing
for cretins—
I wanna yack!

ARROWS OF EROS

Sparrows
dart over
the dark earth,

settle
on apple
boughs in sunlight.

WHAT TO DO?

Something about her
makes me
tits.

NO HARBOR

    Night
    black wind
    digging ocean graves.

PROMISE

Let me
be your Buddha
baby,

skim
the blossoms from
your tree.

INVITATION

    After
    the feast
    you wanna split?

LAMENT

Every
time I
sleep with you

I
dream I
am a virgin.

MIGHTY APHRODITE

Just
another naked
godess riding bareback.

EROS, COME ON,

   speak
   your ancient
   native language—I

   want
   the pleasures
   of your tongue.

RASH

How
it itches,
dawn after dawn,

like
some flea-
infected goat skin.

Pray
to Zeus
it gets gone

soon—
I haven't
fucked in weeks.

CHASTE ARTEMIS

Artemis
among mountains
at bare-chested dawn...

Eros
will have
to thrill himself.

HESPEROS

Star
of stars,
flickerer of dreams,

flit
your fingers
across my lamb.

THEME

    Silver
    stars around
    the silver moon.

MISS SCARLET

Pinot noir scars
soft goat-
hair

skin—big brown-
eyed nipples
pop.

NIGHTINGALE

Sweet-singing
nightingale, dusty
harbinger of spring.

ENOUGH

Suntanning
summer. Cicadas
bitch and moan.

TWO DOVES

Spirits
cold. Wings
flap. Like stone.

DAWN

steps
down in
her gold Stilettos.

ADVICE FOR A GIRL

    Adorn
    your hair
    yellower than fire

    with two white
    flowers, nothing
    more.

TO A YOUNG LOVE

Remember
when we
were whatever beautiful

creatures
we imagined
roaming our wilderness ...

Soft-spoken
cocksure lover,
you deserved laurels!

VISTA

    Woman
    picking wildflowers,
    blouse falling open.

CHAMBER PEEKING

    Soft
    tanned feet
    lifting through air . . .

    tightly
    locking her
    legs around his.

VIRGIN I

Apple
ripe, but
out of reach.

VIRGIN II

    Mountain
    hyacinth trampled
    under shepherd's feet.

MOON HONEY DRIFT

She
could sing
all night long

in
her open
violet bride gown.

We
will be
like honey-voiced nightingales

who
barely sleep
and shrug-off dawn.

END OF THE NIGHT

    a sensual sorrow
    wet skin
    snow

    dawn
    breaks in
    an hour so

    come on again
    again let's
    go

BY MYSELF

    round
    midnight the
    moon's bright eye

    opens,
    the Pleiades
    bare their breasts.

    Hours
    spiraling, I
    sleep with air.

EMPTINESS

Ariyana,
please stop
picking your nose.

MORNING WOOD

Eros
came down
from the mountain

in purple cape
and nothing
else,

penis
jutting out,
a crimson stake.

LOVE GUSTS

Pummeling
mountain oaks,
the relentless wind.

TO EROS

    You
    burn us
    and you laugh.

LATE

    What
    took you
    so long? Now

    Dinner's
    cold and
    tastes like shit.

LOVE

    your goat herd
    should trample
    my

    field—a rose
    for your
    longing

    that I could
    lick your
    sweat

OH

    legs
    both lifted
    over sweaty limbs

ON EARTH

    Loving
    a god's
    easy as breathing;

    loving
    the town's
    most voluptuous gal,

    you
    could die
    or go mad.

IN TRUTH

can't
argue with
a voluptuous gal

TO A CHARMER

How
could I
refuse your desire

unless
I should
desire someone more?

CHOOSING

Couldn't
care less
about the honey,

let alone the
busy little
honeybee...

but
you don't
believe me, huh?

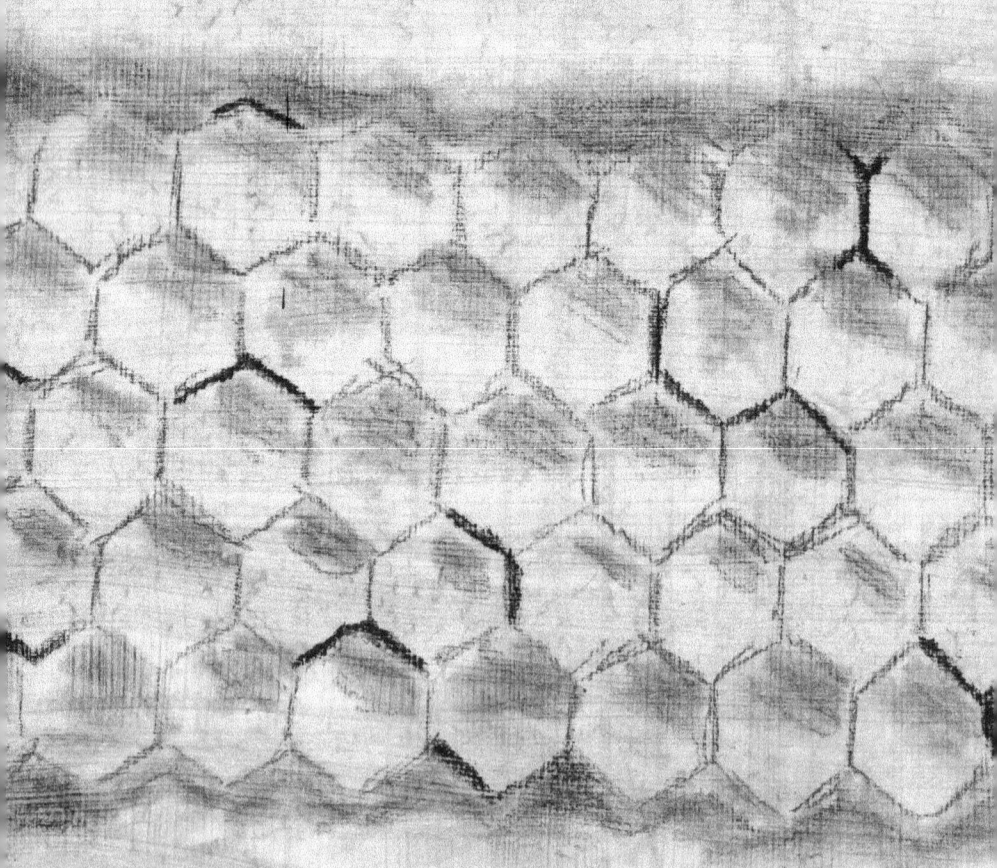

HANDSOME GUY

Stand
up and
look at me,

let me see
your wandering
eyes.

FLIRTING

Chitchat
pleasures
of the tongue—

boys
and girls
can't get enough.

PEEK-A-BOO

Tried
to hide
behind the laurel,

but
your boobs
gave you away.

Watching
you step
out smiling, all

stride
and sheer
white garments flowing,

I
tremble I
want you bad.

REUNION

    Like
    a little
    girl to her

    mother,
    I came
    running to you.

FURY

What
happened to
your sweet tongue?

Now
it moves
in violent clucks,

makes
my body
sticks and stone.

THE RING

    Yes,
    it's big,
    but is he?

HEAD'S UP

    Drive
    me crazy,
    I might scratch

    the nightingale's song
    into your
    ass.

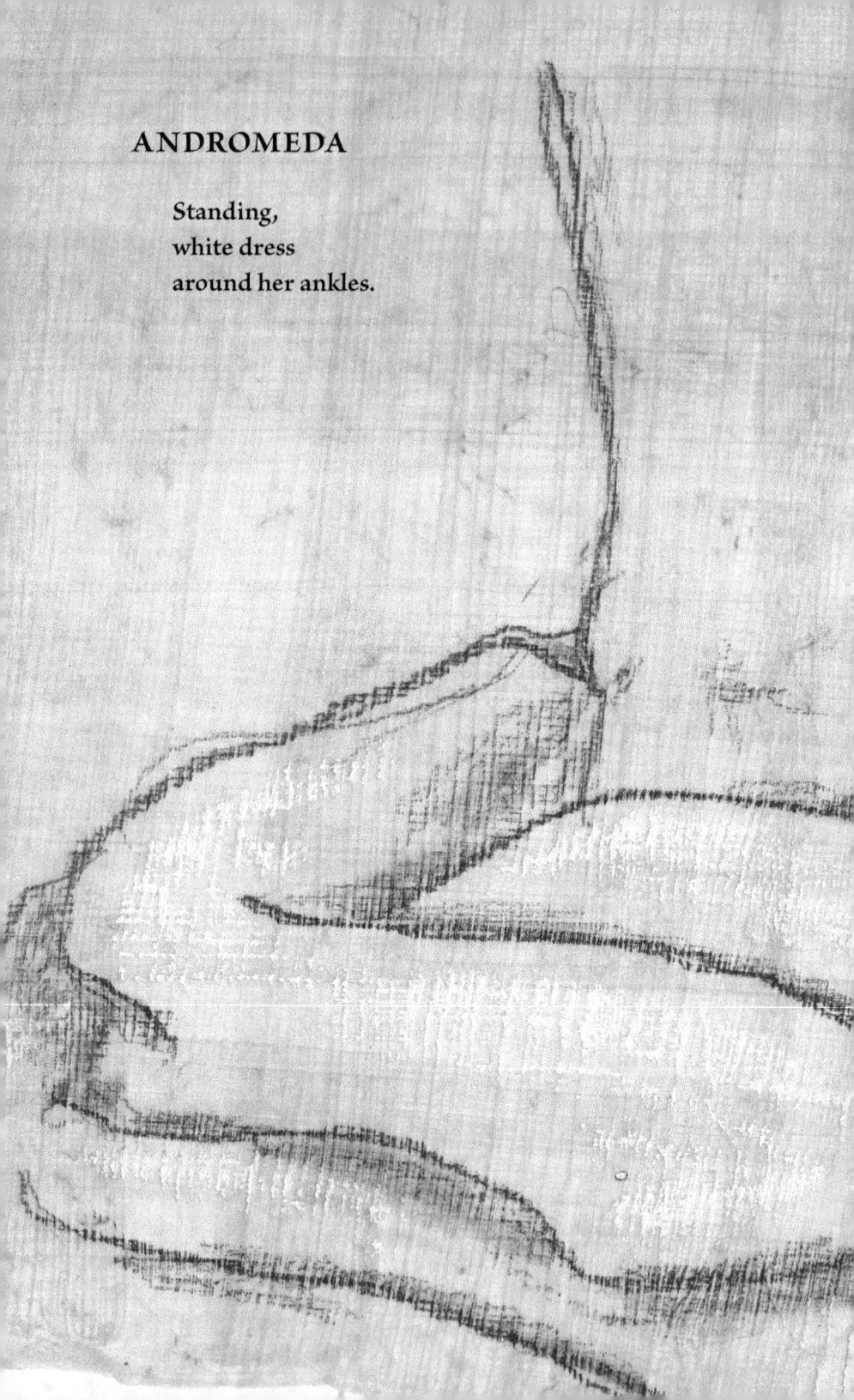

ANDROMEDA

Standing,
white dress
around her ankles.

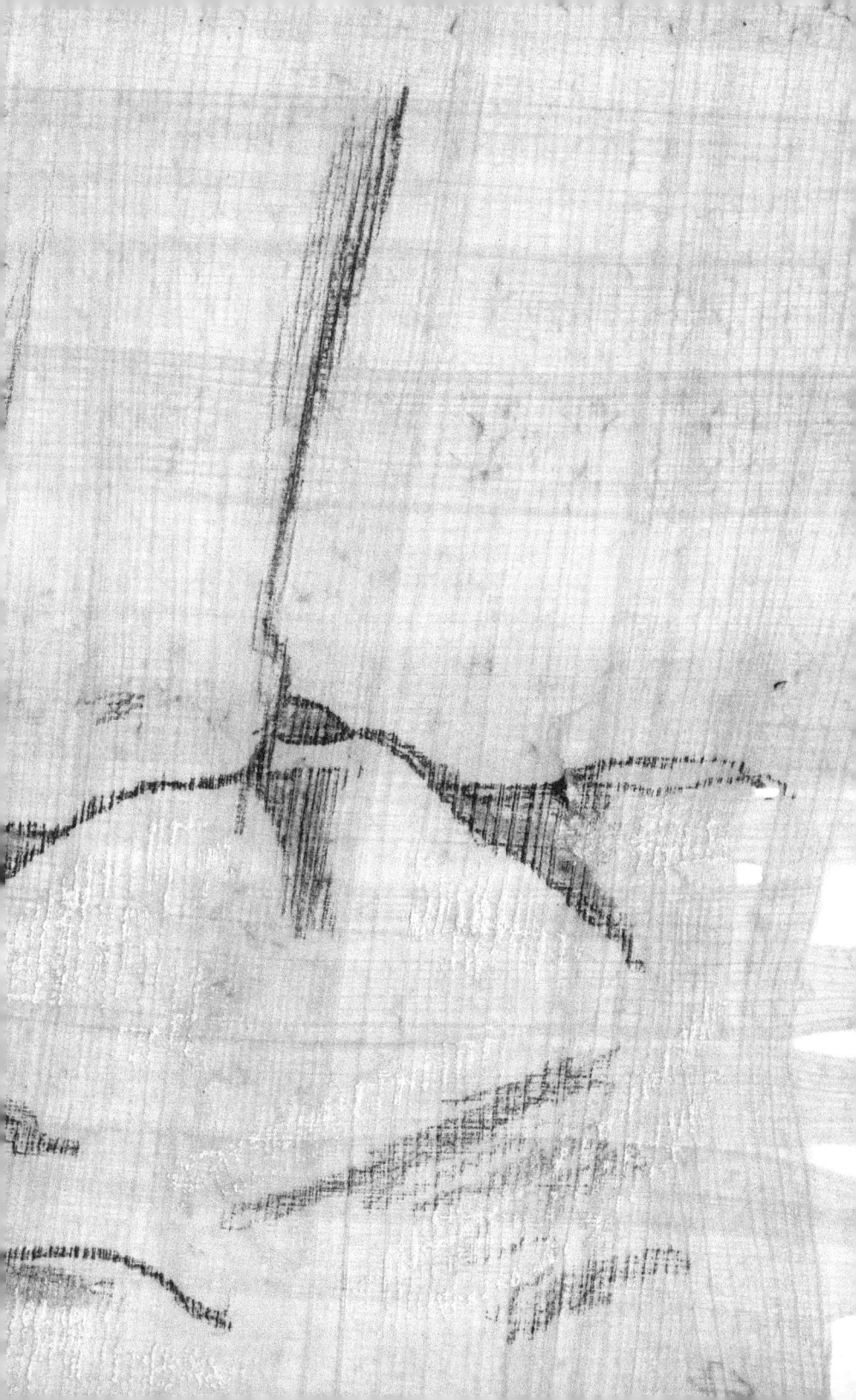

POOR GIRL

    Waif,
    come here,
    I'll take you

    in,
    show you
    around my place.

GRACES, MUSES

I'm not sure
which I
prefer,

the Graces in
their affection
or

the Muses with
their stylish
hair.

PARTING GIFT

Wipe
your semen
with this Kleenex.

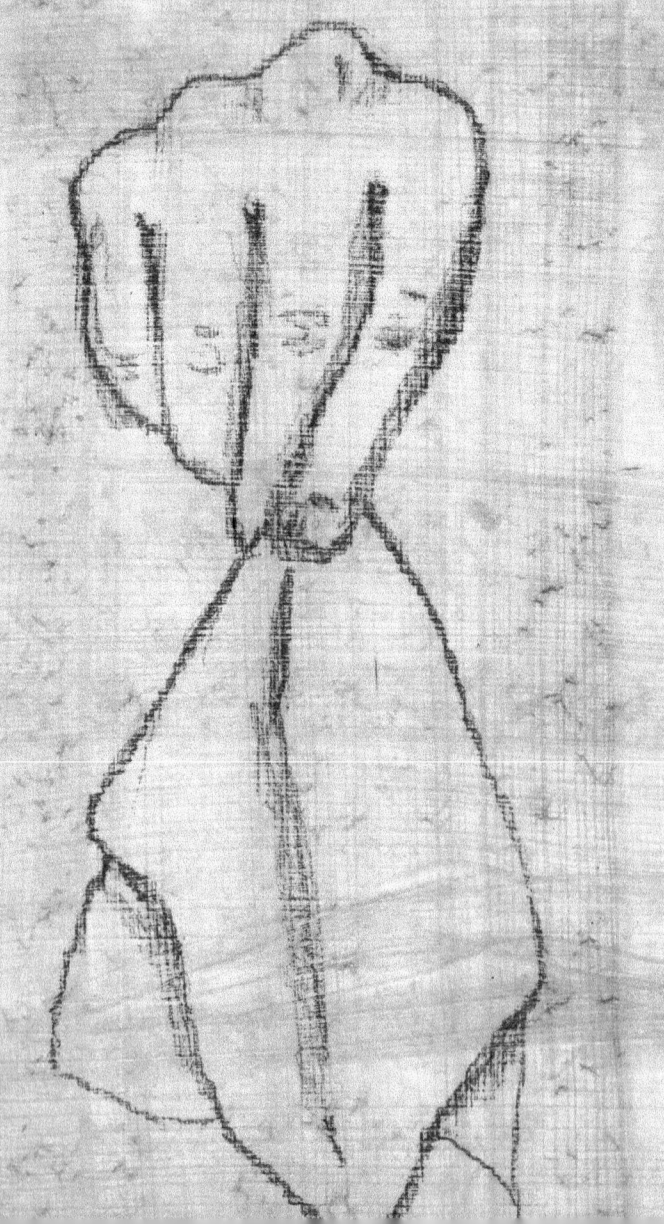

STRANGERS IN THE NIGHT

Your voice
sweeter
than the sound

swinging from
the most delicate
guitar.

Your eyes
whiter
than egg shells—

will they crack
open for
me?

LYRIC FOR LESBOS

    Leg
    around leg
    around leg around

    leg
    around song
    around leg around

    mountain
    of leg
    around leg around

    leg
    around leg
    mountain of song.

HURT

Wind,
tear him
limb from limb.

THE SWALLOW

King Pandion's daughter
pecking at
me?

A COLUMN OF GOOD THINGS

Saffron
robe, apple
blossom robe, amaranth

robe,
black sake
robe, absinthe robe,

doesn't
really matter:
best is always

white
garlands and
flowing open robe.

SOME GIFT

Purple
silk handkerchiefs
are still handkerchiefs.

SANDAL

Straps
across her
feet like rainbows.

GARMENT

Wrapped
in silk,
she looked rapturous.

Without it, she
looked OK
too.

VISION

    Dawn crosses her
    golden arms,
    rests

    them down on
    the dark
    horizon—

    what she sees
    is what
    happens.

ENTERING THE BLACK OF SLEEP

Eyes
close, like
the night sky.

DIALOGUE

Spoke
with you
in a dream.

"Where
you from?"
I asked. "Cyprus."

"You've
traveled far."
"Call me Ulysses."

"Where
to now?"
"You tell me."

GOOD MORNING

    Aphrodite
    hurling soft
    words of desire . . .

    Dawn's
    rosy folds
    moist with dew.

SLEEP

Your girlfriend's breasts
make great
pillows.

TAINTED LOVE

Eros,
when I
close my eyes

your
eyes shine
back at me.

Beauty
burns love
with godly fever.

OLD PRO

    The old man
    down the
    road

    pays
    good cash
    to get off . . .

    I would fuck
    but not
    suck.

GRIEF COUNSELOR

I know death
blows, my
child.

Let me comfort
you like
prayer.

Undress and move
your smooth
legs

here. Chillax over
my sympathetic
lips,

my gently pulsing
tongue and
fingertips.

OLD AGE

    Wrinkled, I
    still chase and
    cajole

    my smooth-skinned
    lady-friends-to-be
    to consider me

    the grove
    their fingers should
    stroll.

THE WORLD DOES NOT END

Ages
from now
people will speak

about
our love—
what it means—

though
time's hand
erases our names.

THE WORLD DOES NOT END

They should know
what we
have

has little
to do
with your

firm
golden apples
and twinkling star.

HERMES AND THE RIVER

Gondola
rides won't
exist for years,

but they will
be like
this ...

May I kiss
the dewy
lotus

tucked
there on
your river banks?

SWEET GIRL

Dawn's
a push-over,
spreading for anyone.

Even alone, she
rosy fingers
herself,

hoping
it brightens
the loners' days.

RE: THE GODS

They
didn't so
much as blink

let
alone shed
a single tear

while
we declared
our fucking love

they
were busy
bickering over alms.

ON BEAUTY AND AGE

Those
cupcake-breasted Muses
never grow old.

I
could lick
their frosting off.

ON BEAUTY AND AGE

My melon breasts,
now wrinkled
prunes;

my bird-wing hair,
now spider
webs.

ON BEAUTY AND AGE

Once
I turned
heads when dancing

my fawn dance,
now I
fall.

ON BEAUTY AND AGE

Why moan?
All of us
age.

At least
I still have
Eros.

ON BEAUTY AND AGE

    Old men
    get it
    the worst.

    Especially those
    who outlive
    their wives.

YOUTH OF TODAY

Young
again, I'd
do you all.

APPRECIATION

Blazing
sun, thanks
for being there—

helping
me seduce
dozens of virgins!

DESIRE AND SUN

    Great
    shining breast
    of the sun.

    Eros,
    please, don't
    ever untie me.

SAPPHO DOES

Sappho
sits alone
against the tide.

What
Sappho does
is her business.

Sappho
dreams; apples
fall from trees.

Three
girls chase
each other around—

one
is love,
one is freedom,

and
one is
a girl alone.

Where
Sappho goes,
crashing wine-dark throes.

When
Sappho leaves
three girls grieve;

one
is naked,
one is clothed,

and
one is
half of both.

Sappho's
little credo:
To be continued . . .

SAPPHO WRITES AGAIN

SING/SUNG

    Today,
    I shall
    for your pleasure.

    Tomorrow,
    I am
    by Mary Barnard.

IMPLICATION

Death,
you suck,
the gods think;

believing
it, they
do not die.

APHRODITE, MY LADY

Sit
and weave
with me awhile

this thin white
gown for
removing.

GIRLFRIEND

Don't
worry that
I hate you.

EPITHALAMIUM

Lucky groom, you
said, "I
do"

as Hesperos beckons
chance boys
home

your bride now
waits, white
wool

shorn true, all
pink for
you.

MY WORD

Eros,
you strike
me from flint!

BEAUTIFUL

Hawk
wings darken
against the sun—

someday
my books
will be burned.

REMEMBER

    Sun freckles
    the empty
    honey jar—

    I know
    the progeny
    of loss.

A GIFT FOR APHRODITE

"Sappho,"
I said,
"purse your lips,

wind
your watch,
set your snare."

A GIFT FOR APHRODITE II

Really,
what doesn't
a goddess have?

White
clover moon;
half slipped-off sandal.

Wide
walrus eyes;
the long-awaited call.

MIRROR EFFECT

Hair
up, hair
down, I dunno—

dumb
little girl
smacks my cheek.

LEDA'S EGG

One cloud
in the hyacinth
sky.

LONG TIME

Shoot,
man, you
really have grown!

WRAPPED

Take
me today,
take me tomorrow,

take
me every
day—take me

yesterday,
if you
can, you can.

A WANDERING

    Lost
    under your gown's
    various flowers,

    my hands . . .
    sorry,
    you were saying?

CLOSE

    White
    locks, dark
    songs. Some end.

SCOTT KEENEY is the author of four poetry collections. His works have appeared in *Columbia Poetry Review*, *Court Green*, *Mudlark*, *New York Quarterly*, *Poetry East*, and other journals. He lives with his family in Connecticut.

www.ingramcontent.com/pod-product-compliance
Lightning Source LLC
Chambersburg PA
CBHW052100110526
44591CB00013B/2285